# RIGHT TACTICS

# TO

# CONTROL

# YOURSELF!

## Birister Sharma

# Copyright © 2022 Birister Sharma

## All Rights Reserved.

**Dedicated to my loving wife….**

**Pallabi Devi Sharma**

**I surrendered to you, O my Lord……**


**"Om Namah Shivaya"**

# Table of Contents

# One word

You have five main sense organs in your body: your eyes, ears, nose, tongue, and hands. Through your eyes, you can see the wonderful world around you. With your ears, you can hear the enchanting sounds of life. With your nose, you can smell the fragrances of this world. With your tongue, you can taste the sweetness of life. And with your hands, you can touch and feel the beauty of creation.

These five sense organs are among the most precious gifts given to us by Almighty God.

Can you live your life without these precious gifts?

No, never.

It is almost impossible to imagine life without them. They allow us to experience the world in its fullness.

Without eyes, life becomes colorless and filled with darkness. Without ears, life turns silent and still. Without a nose, life becomes odorless. Without a tongue, life loses its taste. Without hands, life becomes helpless and incomplete.

But do you know who truly controls these five sense organs in your life?

Obviously—you.

Only you have the power to control them. You are the true controller and guardian of your senses. Without your consent, they cannot act or move in any direction.

Now imagine what would happen if you failed to control them.

If your senses are left uncontrolled, they begin to wander aimlessly. Your eyes may look at things that are not good for you. Your ears may listen to harmful words. Your nose may seek unpleasant things. Your tongue may crave what is unhealthy. Your hands may engage in actions that lead you away from the right path.

Gradually, these uncontrolled senses can bring turmoil into your life in the form of anger, hatred, jealousy, lust, greed, and ego. And this may become the beginning of your downfall.

Therefore, to maintain harmony and balance in life, you must learn to control your senses.

Never allow your senses to lead you blindly.
Never allow them to guide you senselessly.
Never allow them to drive you recklessly.

Instead, you must lead your senses.
You must guide them.
You must direct them wisely.

Your life is like a chariot.

You are the charioteer of your own life.
Your senses are like the horses that pull the chariot.

You are the master of your senses, and they are your servants.

Only you can control them.
Only you can rule them.

Treat them wisely and guide them carefully, and they will always serve you faithfully.

***

# 1. Control Your Mind

**"Once you have control over your mind, anything you want becomes possible."**

Once, there lived a very strange bird in a deep forest. It had two heads but only one body. It was a two-headed bird.

The right head was wise and thoughtful, while the left head was selfish and foolish. The right head always tried to guide the left head with wise advice. He helped him and cared for him like a brother.

However, the left head did not like the suggestions of the right head. Instead, he hated him like his worst enemy. In his heart, he was always planning how to get rid of the right head. Many times he even thought of destroying him through evil means.

But the right head never held any hatred. He always treated the left head with kindness, as his own brother and companion.

As time passed, the hatred in the left head continued to grow. Yet the right head remained unaware of these feelings.

One day, while flying in search of food, the two-headed bird reached another forest. There they saw many bright red berries hanging from the branches.

"Look! What delicious berries those are!" the left head said excitedly. His mouth began to water at the sight of them. He could hardly control his temptation.

The left head wanted to eat the berries immediately, but the right head stopped him.

"No," said the right head cautiously. "We must not eat those berries."

"Why not?" the left head asked angrily.

"Can't you see that those berries are wild and poisonous?"

"How can you say that?" the left head replied. "Can you prove it?"

"Look closely," the right head explained. "There are no ants or insects on those berries. That means they are poisonous."

But the left head refused to listen.

"I don't believe you," he shouted. "I will eat those berries at any cost. You cannot stop me."

The right head tried once again to warn him.

"If we eat those poisonous berries, we will die. Please try to understand."

But his words were useless.

"Fine! You don't eat them if you don't want to," the left head said stubbornly. "But I will."

Finally, the left head forced the bird to move closer to the berries. The right head felt helpless and deeply upset, but he could not stop him.

The moment the left head took the first bite, he suddenly felt dizzy and weak.

"What is happening to me? Why am I feeling so dizzy?" the left head asked in fear.

"I feel the same," replied the right head sadly. "We are both dying now, brother."

"I am very sorry," cried the left head. "I should have listened to you."

"It is too late to regret now," the right head said softly before closing his eyes.

Within moments, the two-headed bird died.

**Moral of the Story**

• There is tremendous power in your mind.
• The way you treat your mind determines how it treats you.
• If you learn to control your mind and guide it in the right direction, it can create wonders in your life.
• But if you fail to control it, your mind can lead you toward downfall and failure.
• If you can control your mind, you can achieve great things in life.
• Never allow your mind to control you.
• Instead, learn to control your mind.
• Be the master of your mind, not its slave.
• Do not live your life in confusion or indecision.
• Always keep your thoughts clear before taking action.
• Believe in yourself and rely on your own strength.

**Ways to Control Your Mind**

• Do not make your mind like the two-headed bird.
• Listen to your conscience.
• Never act without proper thinking and planning.
• Do not allow your mind to wander aimlessly.
• Never let your mind remain idle, because an idle mind becomes a playground for negative thoughts.
• Use your mind for good and meaningful purposes.
• Utilize your mind for growth and self-development.

• Use the power of your mind to accomplish something great.
• Guide your mind toward the right path.
• Lead your mind in the proper direction.
• Train your mind to perform creative and constructive work.
• Do not fill your mind with negative thoughts.
• Always nourish your mind with positive thoughts.

**Arjuna: "For the mind is restless, turbulent, obstinate and very strong, O Krsna, and to subdue it, I think, is more difficult than controlling the wind."**

**Lord Krishna: "O mighty-armed son of Kunti, it is undoubtedly very difficult to curb the restless mind, but it is possible by suitable practice and by detachment.**

**---Bhagavad Gita**

‿***‿

# 2. *Control Your Thoughts*

**"Control your thoughts; otherwise they will control you."**

Once, a man was traveling a long distance for business. His journey had been successful, and he had earned a good amount of money. He felt very happy and satisfied.

On his way back home, he had to pass through a dense forest. The day was hot and humid, and after walking for many hours, he became extremely tired and hungry.

After a long walk, he decided to stop for some rest and have his meal. He sat down under a large shady tree. As he looked around, he suddenly noticed the skeleton of a dead tiger lying nearby.

A frightening thought crossed his mind.

"What if this dead tiger suddenly comes back to life?" he wondered. "What if it attacks me?"

Fear filled his heart.

What the man did not know was that the tree under which he was resting was a **wishing tree**. Whatever anyone wished for while sitting beneath its shade would instantly come true.

The moment the man imagined the dead tiger coming back to life, the impossible happened.

The dead tiger suddenly came alive.

Within seconds, the tiger attacked the frightened man and killed him.

Thus, the poor man lost his life because of his own fearful thoughts.


**Moral of the Story**

- You are the producer of your own thoughts.
- You are also the product of your own thoughts.
- You can create both good and bad thoughts.
- You can create both positive and negative thoughts.
- Your thoughts can make you great.
- Your thoughts can make you small.
- Your thoughts can make you brave and confident.
- Your thoughts can also make you fearful and weak.
- Your thoughts can make you strong.
- Your thoughts can make you powerless.
- Your thoughts can make you prosperous.
- Your thoughts can make you poor in spirit.
- Your thoughts shape your personality and your life.
- Everything in life begins with a thought.
- Your thoughts are the seeds of your desires and actions.
- There is tremendous power in your thoughts.
- Your thoughts can transform imagination into reality.
- Your thoughts can build your life.
- Your thoughts can also destroy your life.
- Ultimately, you become what you consistently think.


**Good Thoughts**

- Think positively about yourself.
- Think encouraging and uplifting thoughts.
- Think great and inspiring ideas.
- Think about creativity and new possibilities.
- Think about the well-being of others.
- Avoid filling your mind with weakness or mediocrity.
- Think about your growth and self-development.
- Fill your mind with thoughts of love, compassion, peace, happiness, friendship, and prosperity.

## Bad Thoughts

- Thinking negatively about yourself.
- Filling your mind with pessimistic thoughts.
- Thinking about destructive or harmful ideas.
- Focusing on the faults of others.
- Allowing weakness and mediocrity to dominate your mind.
- Thinking about hurting others.
- Filling your mind with hatred, anger, jealousy, and envy.

## The Right Way to Control Your Thoughts

- Welcome good thoughts into your mind.
- Do not allow harmful thoughts to stay in your mind.
- Encourage noble and uplifting thoughts.
- Reject evil or destructive thoughts.
- Cultivate positive thinking.
- Avoid negative thinking.
- Develop strong and empowering thoughts.
- Do not entertain weak or discouraging thoughts.
- Nourish your mind with rich and meaningful ideas.
- Avoid thoughts that limit your potential.

**"For one whose mind is unbridled, self-realization is difficult work. But he whose mind is controlled and who strives by appropriate means is assured of success. That is My opinion."**

**---Bhagavad Gita**

⹁***⹁

# 3. Control Your Emotions

**"Don't let your emotions distract you from doing what needs to be done. Control your emotions so they do not control you."**

Raghu was a notorious criminal. He had robbed many people and had even killed several. He had also carried out numerous bank robberies in different areas. His criminal activities had spread fear among the people.

For many years, the police tried to arrest him but failed. Raghu was extremely clever and cunning. He often disguised himself in different appearances, making it almost impossible for anyone to recognize him.

However, after many relentless efforts, the police finally succeeded in capturing him.

After his arrest, Raghu was brought before the court.

"Raghu," the judge said firmly, "you have committed many serious crimes. Now you must face the punishment for them."

The judge then asked, "Do you accept your crimes?"

Raghu remained silent for a moment.

"No, my lord," he finally replied calmly. "I do not accept my crimes."

The judge was surprised by his response. Everyone in the courtroom was stunned. Murmurs spread among the people present.

"Order! Order!" the judge said. "Please maintain silence."

Then the judge looked at Raghu with curiosity.

"Why do you deny your crimes?" the judge asked.

"My lord," Raghu replied confidently, "I did not commit these crimes alone. Before punishing me, you should first punish my mother, because she is the real reason behind my crimes."

The courtroom fell silent again.

Raghu continued, "If my mother had stopped me when I stole something for the first time as a child, I would not have become a criminal today. I would not be standing before you as a convict. Therefore, she is the real culprit."

The judge paused for a moment and then asked, "Is Raghu's mother present in the courtroom?"

An old woman wearing a white sari slowly stepped forward into the witness box. Tears were streaming down her face.

"Are you Raghu's mother?" the judge asked.

"Yes, my lord," she replied with trembling voice. "I am the unfortunate mother of Raghu."

"Would you like to say something about your son?" the judge asked gently.

The old woman sobbed for a moment before speaking.

"My lord, whatever Raghu has said is true. I am responsible for his crimes. I failed as a mother. When he made mistakes in his childhood, I did not correct him. I was too emotional and too attached to him."

She continued through tears.

"Whenever he did something wrong, I ignored it because of my excessive love and affection. I was afraid that if I scolded or punished him, he might leave me. I could not control my emotions. My blind attachment ruined his life."

"My lord, please punish me for my failure as a mother."

After saying this, the old woman collapsed in the witness box.

The next day, Raghu was sentenced to death for his terrible crimes.


**Moral of the Story**

• Uncontrolled emotions can lead to grief, anxiety, and stress.
• Excessive emotional attachment can cloud judgment.
• When emotions dominate your decisions, it becomes difficult to act wisely.
• Life requires both compassion and practical thinking.
• Important decisions should be guided by wisdom, not by uncontrolled emotions.
• Do not allow your emotions to overpower your sense of responsibility.

**Ways to Control Your Emotions**

• Do not let your emotions carry you away.
• Do not become blind with attachment and sentiment.
• Avoid making decisions purely out of emotion.
• Be practical and thoughtful in your actions.
• Think carefully before you act.
• Balance love and discipline in your relationships.
• Do not allow emotional attachment to make you forget your responsibilities.
• Show love, affection, and compassion, but within healthy limits.
• Never allow emotional impulses to block your path to success.
• Learn to balance your emotions with wisdom and reality.


**"O son of Pandu, he who does not hate illumination, attachment and delusion when they are present or long for them when they disappear; who is unwavering and undisturbed**

through all these reactions of the material qualities, remaining neutral and transcendental, knowing that the modes alone are active; who is situated in the self and regards alike happiness and distress; who looks upon a lump of earth, a stone and a piece of gold with an equal eye; who is equal toward the desirable and the undesirable; who is steady, situated equally well in praise and blame, honor and dishonor; who treats alike both friend and enemy; and who has renounced all material activities- such a person is said to have transcended the modes of nature."

---Bhagavad Gita

⁓***⁓

# 4. *Control Your Actions*

**"You can control your actions, but not their results."**

Once there were two brothers named Mohanlal and Sohanlal who lived in a small village. Mohanlal was the elder brother.

Mohanlal was not a rich man, but he was humble, kind, and honest. He always helped the people in the village. Whenever someone came to him for help, he never refused. Even if it meant giving away his own share of money or possessions, he was willing to do so for the welfare of the poor.

He was known as a true friend of the poor. Because of his good deeds and generous nature, everyone in the village loved and respected him.

On the other hand, Sohanlal was a very rich man, but his nature was completely different from that of his elder brother. He was arrogant, dishonest, and corrupt. Instead of helping people, he often cheated the poor. He cared only about his own profit and comfort.

Because of his bad behavior, people in the village disliked and avoided him. His name became associated with selfishness and wrongdoing.

Years passed, and one day both brothers died.

When Mohanlal passed away, the entire village gathered to pay their respects. His funeral was conducted with great honor. People mourned his death and prayed for his soul. Many villagers attended his last rites, remembering the kindness and generosity he had shown throughout his life.

However, the situation was very different when Sohanlal died.

No one from the village came to attend his funeral. No one mourned his death. No one organized prayers in his memory. Only his wife and sons were present at his final rites.

Thus, the way people remembered the two brothers reflected the kind of lives they had lived.

**Moral of the Story**

• Your actions define the true character of your life.
• Nothing meaningful happens without action.
• One right action can uplift your life, while one wrong action can damage it.
• Actions speak louder than words.
• Your actions shape the results you experience.
• Your actions determine your success or failure.
• Good actions build a noble personality, while bad actions damage it.
• Good actions often lead to positive outcomes, while bad actions bring negative consequences.

**Your Good Actions**

• Good actions lead you toward goodness and greatness.
• Good actions support and uplift you in life.
• Good actions open the door to success and honor.
• Good actions earn you love and respect from others.
• Good actions build meaningful friendships and strong relationships.
• Good actions make you humble and generous.
• Good actions develop responsibility and integrity.
• Good actions multiply joy, happiness, and prosperity.

**Your Bad Actions**

• Bad actions lead to pain and mediocrity.
• Bad actions rarely bring lasting benefit.
• Bad actions often lead to downfall and failure.
• Bad actions attract hatred and disrespect.
• Bad actions make a person lonely and isolated.
• Bad actions promote arrogance and selfishness.
• Bad actions weaken responsibility and character.
• Bad actions multiply worries, anxiety, and stress.


**Ways to Guide Your Actions**

• Think carefully before taking action.
• Work with courage and integrity.
• Be honest with yourself and with others.
• Remain loyal to your values and principles.
• Respect others just as you respect yourself.
• Never forget your responsibilities in life.
• Do what is right for yourself and beneficial for others.
• Treat everyone with kindness and dignity.
• Avoid hurting anyone emotionally, mentally, or physically.
• Spread love, compassion, and goodwill wherever you go.
• Let your actions demonstrate your character.
• Live by the simple principle: **"Be good and do good."**


**"Abandoning all attachment to the results of his activities,
ever satisfied and independent, he performs no fruitive action,
although engaged in all kinds of undertakings."**

**---Bhagavad Gita**


⌒***⌒

# 5. Control Your Habits

**"Take control of your habits; take control of your life."**

Once there was a huge banyan tree in a forest. It was the home of many birds, tiny insects, and small creatures. During hot and humid days, it also offered shade like a great umbrella to travelers passing through the forest.

All the creatures living in the banyan tree were happy and content. The banyan tree also enjoyed their company and treated them like its own family.

Time passed peacefully. With every changing season, new birds, insects, and small creatures came and made the tree their home. They lived together happily.

One day, a small seed of a nut was carried by the wind and fell into a hollow in the trunk of the banyan tree.

The banyan tree felt irritated by the presence of the small seed.

"O dear little seed," said the banyan tree gently, "please leave my trunk. Your presence is troubling me."

"O mighty and gracious banyan tree," replied the small seed politely, "I am only a tiny seed. How could I trouble someone as great as you? If I have caused you discomfort, I sincerely apologize."

Then the seed pleaded, "Please allow me to stay here only for this windy and dry season. I am afraid of the harsh weather. Once the season passes, I will surely leave."

The banyan tree finally agreed.

But when the windy season passed, the seed did not leave.

The summer passed, but the seed still remained.

Then winter, autumn, and spring also passed, yet the seed continued to stay inside the trunk of the banyan tree.

Slowly, the tiny seed began to grow into a small seedling.

"O dear seed," said the banyan tree again, "you have now grown into a small plant inside my trunk. Your roots are beginning to hurt me. Please leave."

"O mighty banyan tree," replied the seedling calmly, "why are you worried about my tiny roots? They are just baby roots. They will not harm you. Please do not worry."

Time continued to pass.

Years later, the small seedling grew into a large tree inside the trunk of the banyan tree. Its roots spread deeper and stronger, eventually destroying the banyan tree that had once given it shelter.

Thus, the mighty banyan tree died because it allowed the tiny seed to grow inside it.


**Moral of the Story**

• Every habit begins small, just like a tiny seed.
• If you allow it to grow unchecked, it can eventually become powerful enough to shape your life.
• Good habits can build your life.
• Bad habits can slowly destroy it.
• What starts as something small can eventually become something that controls you.

**Your Good Habits**

- Good habits help build a meaningful life.
- Good habits help you develop a strong career.
- Good habits nurture your character and integrity.
- Good habits guide you toward the right path.
- Good habits help you become a better person.
- Good habits bring happiness and contentment.
- Good habits make you disciplined and responsible.
- Good habits lead you toward success.

**Your Bad Habits**

- Bad habits slowly spoil your life.
- Bad habits can destroy your career.
- Bad habits weaken your character.
- Bad habits lead you toward poor choices.
- Bad habits push you in the wrong direction.
- Bad habits make you unhappy and dissatisfied.
- Bad habits make you careless and irresponsible.
- Bad habits often lead to failure.

Your habits ultimately reveal your personality.

If you cultivate good habits, you improve your life. But if you cultivate bad habits, you damage your life.

It is very easy to develop bad habits, but it is extremely difficult to remove them once they become strong.

**The Right Ways to Control Your Habits**

• Do not allow bad habits to grow within you.
• Remove harmful habits before they take deep root.
• Always develop positive habits in your life.
• Practice and cultivate good habits consistently.
• Remember that bad habits can silently destroy your life.
• Bad habits are like hidden enemies.
• They slowly weaken your strengths.
• They act like parasites that feed on your best qualities.
• Bad habits can eventually lead you toward destruction.
• Stay aware of your habits and guide them wisely.

**"The senses are so strong and impetuous, O Arjuna, that they forcibly carry away the mind even of a man of discrimination who is endeavoring to control them."**

**"One who restrains his senses, keeping them under full control and fixes his consciousness upon Me, is known as a man of steady intelligence."**

**---Bhagavad Gita**

᷍***᷍

# 6. Control Your Desires and Wishes

**"Your desires and wishes are the wings of your life; control them before they control you."**

Once there was a man who lived happily in a small house. Though his life was simple, he was peaceful and content. He was known as an honest and kind person. People in the neighborhood loved and respected him. He had many friends and well-wishers.

However, one day a new desire entered his mind. He began to wish for a bigger house, even though his income was modest and his needs were already fulfilled. Deep inside, he knew that it was an unnecessary desire.

In order to fulfill this wish, he decided to earn more money. Gradually, he started using unfair means to increase his wealth. Eventually, he managed to earn enough money and built a large house.

But his desires did not stop there.

After some time, he dreamed of building an even bigger mansion. To fulfill this new desire, he needed far more money than before. Once again, he turned to illegal and dishonest methods. This time he crossed every moral boundary.

Soon, he built a magnificent mansion.

However, when he finally began living in his luxurious mansion, he discovered something unexpected—his happiness had disappeared.

His mind was filled with anxiety, fear, and stress because of the wrong actions he had taken. His conscience no longer allowed him to live peacefully.

Then he realized something important: he had been far happier when he lived in his small house.

His uncontrolled desires had pushed him toward dishonesty and wrongdoing. Slowly, people began to hate and disrespect him. His friends abandoned him. Even his loved ones distanced themselves.

He was left alone in his grand mansion.

The life that once felt like heaven had now turned into a living hell. Every day he lived with fear, guilt, and loneliness—like a prisoner of his own actions.

**Moral of the Story**

• Be happy and content with what you have in life.
• Control unnecessary desires and excessive wishes.
• Learn to control your temptations.
• Do not be carried away by the urge for instant gratification.
• Think carefully before making major decisions.
• Live a balanced and thoughtful life.
• Do not forget your moral duties and responsibilities.
• True happiness comes from within, not from material possessions.

**Ways to Control Your Desires and Wishes**

• Understand the nature of your desires.
• Do not allow your desires to cross healthy limits.
• Do not let your desires become wild or uncontrolled.
• Remember that human desires can easily become endless.
• Desires are like untamed beasts—they can wander anywhere if left uncontrolled.
• Guide your desires in the right direction.

- Keep them aligned with your values and principles.
- Never allow your desires to dominate your life.
- Learn to control your desires with wisdom and discipline.
- If you fail to control them, they may lead you into serious trouble.

**"While contemplating the objects of the senses, a person develops attachment for them, and from such attachment lust develops, and from lust anger arises."**

**---Bhagavad Gita**

‿***‿

# 7. Control Your Anger

**"Control your anger; it's only one letter away from danger."**

Once there lived a sage named Durbasha. He was a great and enlightened sage, but he was also known for his extremely angry nature.

Whenever someone disrespected him or disobeyed his command, he would immediately curse that person. Because of this, people feared him greatly—even the gods of heaven were afraid of his anger. His temper had become famous everywhere.

As time passed, Durbasha went deep into the forest to perform intense meditation. Years went by while he remained absorbed in his spiritual practice. In his deep meditation, he had almost forgotten about his family.

After many years, Durbasha finally returned home. On his way back, he became very thirsty. Soon he saw a well nearby. Sitting beside the well was a young woman.

"O young lady," Durbasha said politely, "please give me some water. I am very thirsty. May God bless you."

He asked her once.
He asked her twice.
He asked her three times.

But the young woman did not respond.

In truth, she had not heard him. She was lost in her thoughts, remembering her beloved husband who had gone far away and had left her alone. At that time she was pregnant and living in deep worry and loneliness.

Durbasha felt insulted.

His anger flared up immediately.

"You disobedient girl!" he shouted in rage. "Whoever you are thinking about right now will forget you from this very moment. This is my curse to you!"

He sprinkled water from his *kamandal* (water pot) upon her as he spoke the curse.

Startled, the young woman suddenly realized that someone was standing beside her.

"O great sage," she pleaded humbly, bowing before him, "please forgive me. If I have unknowingly disobeyed you, I sincerely apologize."

Durbasha was surprised by her gentle behavior.

At that moment another woman came running toward them and fell at the sage's feet.

"O great sage," she cried, "what have you done? Why did you curse her?"

Durbasha looked confused.

Then the woman spoke again.

"She is your daughter."

The woman was none other than Durbasha's wife.

The sage was stunned.

"She is... our daughter?" Durbasha said in deep sorrow. Only then did he realize the terrible mistake he had made.

"O God," he cried, "what have I done?"

But the curse could not be taken back.

Durbasha sat in meditation for some time and then gave a blessing to soften the curse. He declared that whenever his daughter expressed her true love to her husband, he would remember her again and they would be reunited.

From that day forward, Durbasha made a vow that he would never again allow anger to control him, and he would never curse anyone in anger.

Years later, when the young woman's son had grown into a strong and handsome young man, she was finally reunited with her husband.

**Moral of the Story**

• Anger is one of the most destructive emotions in human life.
• Uncontrolled anger can burn not only your life but also the lives of others around you.
• Anger often becomes the source of many problems and regrets.
• If you do not control your anger quickly, it can destroy your peace and happiness.
• Always remember: **anger is only one letter away from danger.**

**Ways to Control Your Anger**

• Keep your mind calm and composed.
• Do not expect too much from others.
• Always think carefully before reacting.
• Do not make decisions when you are emotionally disturbed.
• Avoid jumping to conclusions too quickly.
• Give yourself time to think before taking action.
• Act only when your mind, body, and heart are in harmony.
• Remember that you are not always right.
• Try to see situations from the perspective of others.
• Focus on solutions rather than problems.
• Anger never solves problems—it only creates more.

- Everyone makes mistakes.
- Learn to accept your own mistakes.
- Practice forgiveness and let go of resentment.

27

"From anger, complete delusion arises, and from delusion bewilderment of memory. When memory is bewildered, intelligence is lost, and when intelligence is lost one falls down again into the material pool."

---Bhagavad Gita

⌣***⌣

# 8. Control Your Hatred

**"Your hatred only poisons your mind, body, and soul. Control your hatred before it ruins your beautiful life."**

In the great epic *Mahabharata*, Shakuni—the maternal uncle of Duryodhana—planted the seeds of hatred in Duryodhana's mind against the Pandavas.

Duryodhana began to hate his cousin brothers—the Pandavas—so intensely that he constantly plotted against them. His heart was filled with jealousy and bitterness. Time and again, he devised conspiracies to harm them and treated them like his greatest enemies.

One of his first schemes was the **Lakshagriha conspiracy**, in which he attempted to burn the Pandavas—Yudhisthira, Bhima, Arjuna, Nakula, and Sahadeva—along with their mother Kunti alive in a palace made of flammable materials. However, the Pandavas managed to escape from this deadly trap.

But Duryodhana did not stop.

He later organized a deceitful **game of dice**, designed to defeat the Pandavas through unfair means. In that game, the Pandavas lost their kingdom, Indraprastha. During this humiliation, their wife Draupadi was insulted and dragged into the royal court by Dushasana. At that critical moment, Lord Krishna came to her rescue.

As a result of the game, the Pandavas were forced into exile in the forest for thirteen long years.

Despite all the hardships, the Pandavas endured their exile with courage and determination.

After completing the thirteen years of exile, they asked for the return of their rightful kingdom. However, Duryodhana refused to return anything. He was not even willing to grant them five small villages—one for each brother.

His hatred had blinded him completely.

Finally, the great **Mahabharata war** broke out between the Pandavas and the Kauravas.

In the terrible battle that followed, the Kauravas were defeated. Duryodhana not only lost the war but also lost his own life. His ninety-nine brothers were killed, and the entire Kaurava dynasty was destroyed.

Thus, the hatred that once burned in his heart ultimately led to his complete downfall.

**Moral of the Story**

• Hatred is like a disease that slowly destroys a person.
• Once hatred enters your heart, it can damage not only your life but also your relationships.
• Hatred often becomes the root cause of conflicts and divisions.
• As soon as the seed of hatred appears in your heart, remove it immediately.
• Hatred is the greatest enemy of love, compassion, unity, happiness, and peace.

**Ways to Control Hatred**

• Never allow the seeds of hatred to grow within you.
• Remember that hatred often leads to downfall and failure.
• Practice forgiveness and compassion.
• Avoid hurting others intentionally.
• Listen to your conscience rather than being influenced by others.
• Learn to remain happy and content within yourself.
• Do not look at others with envy or jealousy.
• Pray for the well-being of everyone.
• Avoid unnecessary complaints about life.

- Maintain balance in your thoughts and actions.
- Treat others with kindness and respect.
- Do not create divisions in your mind.
- Share love, kindness, and affection with others.
- Remember that every human heart longs for love.
- Appreciate the people around you.
- Do not forget to love and respect yourself.
- Love and compassion are the only ways to win the hearts of others.

**"One who is not envious but is a kind friend to all living entities, who does not think himself a proprietor and is free from false ego, who is equal in both happiness and distress, who is tolerant, always satisfied, self-controlled, and engaged in devotional service with determination, his mind and intelligence fixed on Me- such a devotee of Mine is very dear to Me."**

**---Bhagavad Gita**

⸱***⸱

# 9. Control Your Jealousy

**"Jealousy is when you count someone else's blessings instead of your own."**

Once, in a football team, there was a player named Jackie who became jealous of the star striker, Rocky.

During every match, Jackie behaved like Rocky's opponent rather than his teammate. Whenever he received the ball, he refused to pass it to Rocky. Instead, he deliberately passed it to other players.

Rocky, however, continued to play his natural game. Despite Jackie's jealousy and lack of cooperation, Rocky scored goals in match after match and earned great name and fame.

Seeing Rocky's growing success, Jackie became even more jealous and envious. Slowly, he began losing his own self-belief and confidence. He stopped talking to Rocky and started avoiding him altogether.

Whenever Rocky practiced on the football field, Jackie stayed away. Instead of improving his own skills, Jackie spent his time criticizing Rocky and pointing out his weaknesses.

Gradually, Jackie's performance became weaker and more disappointing in every match.

Frustrated with himself, he turned to drinking alcohol and taking drugs. His physical and mental health began to deteriorate.

Then one day, during an important match, Jackie suddenly collapsed on the field. He was paralyzed and rushed to the hospital.

After he recovered and was released from the hospital, the football club removed his name from the team. His career had ended.

Only then did Jackie realize the terrible mistake he had made. His jealousy had destroyed not only his career but also his life.


## Moral of the Story

• Do not allow jealousy and envy to enter your life.
• Jealousy weakens your self-confidence.
• Jealousy only ruins your happiness and peace.
• When jealousy enters your heart, it begins destroying you first.
• Jealousy is like a poison.
• It poisons your mind, body, and soul.
• It corrupts your thoughts, ideas, decisions, and actions.
• It blocks your growth and personal development.
• If you waste your time being jealous of others, you lose the blessings of your own life.
• Jealousy never leads to success.


## Ways to Control Jealousy

• Never look at others with jealousy.
• Do not compare yourself with anyone.
• Remember that every person is unique and different.
• Be happy and content with what you have.
• Learn to celebrate the success and happiness of others.
• Appreciate and compliment your teammates and friends.
• Motivate and encourage others just as you encourage yourself.
• Learn valuable lessons from the lives of successful people.
• Focus on improving your own abilities.
• Work on developing your own life.
• Do not blindly follow the paths of others.
• Do not compete out of jealousy.
• Instead, challenge yourself to overcome your own difficulties and limitations.

"He who is satisfied with gain which comes of its own accord, who is free from duality and does not envy, who is steady in both success and failure, is never entangled, although performing actions."

---Bhagavad Gita

⌣***⌣

# 10. Control Your Greed

**"Greed is the root cause of all evils. Control it!"**

Once upon a time, there was a king named Vikram who ruled over a vast kingdom. However, he was extremely greedy.

Whenever his subjects came to him seeking help for their problems, King Vikram would first demand gifts from them before agreeing to solve their issues. Because of his greedy nature, his nobles and courtiers were deeply troubled and unhappy.

King Vikram had a little daughter named Phoolmati. She was very sweet and beautiful. The king loved her more than his own life and fulfilled all her wishes. She was his most beloved child.

Despite his greed, King Vikram was a devoted follower of Lord Vishnu. Every day he offered prayers to Lord Vishnu before taking his meal.

One day, while the king was performing his daily prayers, Lord Vishnu appeared before him.

"O King Vikram," Lord Vishnu said, "open your eyes. I am pleased with your devotion."

When King Vikram opened his eyes, he was astonished. For a moment he was speechless, unable to believe that Lord Vishnu was standing before him.

"I want to grant you a boon," said Lord Vishnu kindly. "Ask for whatever you desire."

The king was overwhelmed with excitement.

"O my Lord," King Vikram said eagerly, "please grant me a boon that whatever I touch with my hands turns into gold."

"So be it," Lord Vishnu replied with a smile. After granting the boon, he disappeared in a flash of light.

King Vikram was filled with excitement. There was no limit to his joy. Immediately he began touching everything around him.

And just as he had wished, everything he touched turned into gold.

He was delighted.

Throughout the day, he kept testing his magical power and turned many objects into gold.

After some time, he felt hungry. He saw an apple lying on the table and reached for it. But the moment he touched the apple, it turned into solid gold.

He became frustrated.

Then he ordered his servants to bring him delicious food. The servants served him many dishes, but every time he touched the food, it turned into gold. He could not eat anything.

He shouted in anger and despair, but he was helpless.

The entire day passed like this. Even at night he could not sleep. Fear and tension filled his mind.

The next morning, King Vikram was sitting alone in the garden when his daughter Phoolmati came running toward him.

"Stop! Stop!" the king shouted in panic. "Do not come near me, my dear child!"

But the little girl did not understand. She ran to him and hugged him lovingly.

At that very moment, she turned into a statue of gold.

"O my God!" cried King Vikram in grief. "What have I done?"

He wept bitterly and realized his terrible mistake.

The king immediately ran to the temple of Lord Vishnu and prayed desperately.

"O my Lord," he cried, "please take back your boon. I do not want gold anymore. Please give my daughter back her life."

Lord Vishnu appeared again and restored Phoolmati to her normal form.

From that day onward, King Vikram realized the danger of greed and vowed that he would never again allow greed to control his life.

**Moral of the Story**

• Greed often leads people toward loss and suffering.
• Greed can make a person lose what is truly valuable in life.
• It is not chance or fate that destroys a person's wealth and happiness, but uncontrolled greed.
• Greed blinds a person to wisdom and gratitude.

**Ways to Control Greed**

• Remember that success and growth take time.
• Do not expect instant results in life.
• Learn to practice patience.
• Do not compete blindly with others.
• Focus on improving yourself.
• Avoid taking unnecessary risks.
• If you take risks, make them calculated and thoughtful.
• Understand the balance between risk and reward.
• Always research and think carefully before making decisions.
• Do not be misled by false promises or unrealistic opportunities.
• Be practical and realistic in your life.

- Move forward slowly but consistently.
- Think wisely and act responsibly.
- Save your resources for difficult times.
- Never gamble with your life or future.
- Control your temptations before they control you.

**"There are three gates leading to this hell- lust, anger and greed. Every sane man should give these up, for they lead to the degradation of the soul."**

**---Bhagavad Gita**

⸺***⸺

# 11. Control Your Ego

**"Don't let your ego take control of your life."**

In the great epic *Ramayana*, the demon king Ravana was born into a Brahmin family. He was a highly learned scholar with deep knowledge of the Vedas. Ravana was also a devoted follower of Lord Shiva.

Through his intense penance, he received a powerful boon from Lord Brahma that no god, goddess, demon, or celestial being could kill him.

Because of this boon, Ravana developed immense pride and ego. He believed that no one in the entire universe could defeat him. Gradually, his arrogance grew so strong that he began tormenting people on earth, in heaven, and even in the netherworld.

However, Ravana forgot one important detail: the boon did not protect him from being defeated by a human being.

To restore balance and justice, Lord Vishnu took birth in human form as Lord Rama.

Blinded by arrogance, Ravana committed his greatest mistake. He kidnapped Sita, the wife of Lord Rama, who was the incarnation of Goddess Lakshmi.

Ravana's wise brother Vibhishana repeatedly advised him to return Sita to Lord Rama with respect and honor. But Ravana refused to listen. Instead, driven by his pride and ego, he insulted Vibhishana and banished him from the kingdom of Lanka.

Eventually, a great war took place between Lord Rama and Ravana.

In the fierce battle that followed, Ravana was defeated and killed by Lord Rama.

Ravana's arrogance and ego did not only lead to his own death. It also caused the death of many of his sons and brothers and brought destruction to his magnificent kingdom, the golden city of Lanka.

Thus, Ravana's downfall became a powerful example of how unchecked ego can destroy even the most powerful person.

## Moral of the Story

- Ego is one of the greatest obstacles to wisdom and peace.
- When ego grows, it blinds a person to truth and reason.
- Ego can poison the mind and weaken good judgment.
- Ego destroys relationships, wisdom, and harmony.
- When ego dominates a person's life, downfall eventually follows.
- Arrogance leads to isolation, conflict, and failure.
- A person who cannot control their ego ultimately harms themselves.

## Ways to Control Your Ego

- Practice humility in your life.
- Avoid living with false pride or arrogance.
- Never underestimate others.
- Treat everyone with respect and kindness.
- Remember that no one is superior to everyone else.
- Listen carefully to the advice of your well-wishers.
- Seek guidance from wise and experienced people before making important decisions.
- Avoid surrounding yourself with flatterers who only praise you.
- Stay connected to your moral values and principles.
- Practice generosity and kindness.
- Learn to control excessive desires and pride.

• Evaluate situations carefully before accepting others' opinions.
• Reflect on your actions and behavior every day.

**"A person who has given up all desires for sense gratification, who lives free from desires, who has given up all sense of proprietorship and is devoid of false ego- he alone can attain real peace."**

**---Bhagavad Gita**

**Points to remember:**

• Only you can control yourself.
• No one else has the power to control your life unless you allow it.
• Never allow anyone to dominate or control your decisions.
• Do not become a puppet in the hands of others.
• Only you can control your thoughts.
• Only you can control your mind.
• Only you can control your desires and wishes.
• Only you can control your emotions.
• Only you can control your actions.
• Only you can control your habits.
• Only you can control your anger.
• Only you can control your hatred.
• Only you can control your jealousy.
• Only you can control your greed.

~***~

〜***〜

You are the only person who truly has the power to control your
life.

Take responsibility for your thoughts, your choices, and your
actions.

Be the master of your own life—not the slave of your
weaknesses.

〜***〜

# *About the author:*

Birister Sharma is a full time author. He is also an avid reader. He loves reading, writing, and motivation. He has penned down dozens of self-help motivational books and novels so far.

You may contact him @ birister2007@gmail.com